Ask and Create your Life

Would you be willing to be
the question that changes
the present and the future?

Beate Nimsky

ACCESS
CONSCIOUSNESS
PUBLISHING

German Original published ©2017 Beate Nimsky by BOD – Books on Demand
ISBN: 978-3-7448-4543-4

Coverillustration: rvika©123RF.com
Translation: Corinna Kaebel
Editing: Delany Delaney

ISBN: 978-1-63493-182-3

Published by Access Consciousness Publishing, LLC

Contents

1. The Magic of Asking Questions

We have just been assigned another huge project! I love this kind of challenge. But something in my neck is stiffening up. My schedule is fully booked with a wide variety of assignments, including coachings, seminars, moderating strategic conventions. It really is a nice feeling – so much diversity and so many exciting topics in my life: meeting people, giving advice, support and guidance, thinking in new ways, offering new perspectives, observing how problems are being solved, creating success together.

And now, we go to the new huge project. Our role is one of consulting and supporting in a merger of companies. We are assigned the responsiblity of assisting the chairmen in choosing from eighty executives those co-workers that will be part of creating the new company. This is exactly where my capacities are called for, this project is right up my alley! Yet, one day, amidst of all of these tightly-scheduled appointments requiring my presence, hundreds of kilometers spent on the highway and constantly packing and unpacking my suitcases, I find myself exhausted and fed up.

My beloved morning routine with fitness exercises, meditation, green tea and valuable conversations with my husband has shrunk to a mere 20 minutes or fallen through the cracks altogether. That is, directly under my work desk on top of which are stacks of documents and books piled upon each other!

I have reached my limit. What was once a source of joy has now become a burden. What now? The dates are set. No break in sight until the end of the year. Morning and night I stand in the bathroom, wherever that may be, close my eyes and ask myself aloud: "What can I do different? What can I add, and what can I leave out in order to have fun again?" I actually love working with people and consciousness!

I find an email from Access Consciousness® in my inbox. Obviously I've been on their website or left my address. Sounds interesting. No time to read it though. I create a folder in Outlook and move the email there, and more of its kind. Unread. One day, my sister brings me an article from a small health journal, and says: "Read this". I've been there, she says. It's really interesting, Access Bars® by Access Consciousness®. Okay, I've got it. If, after having addressed questions into the universe for weeks now, I have something show up even physically on my desk this must mean something. I realize that I had asked and kept asking and the answer had been there all along!

My inner journey with Access Consciousness has begun. In 2015, I spend 30 days in seminars with Gary Douglas and Dr. Dain Heer. I follow them to Australia, New Zealand, Denver, Stockholm, Vienna and in Costa Rica I become a Certified Facilitator. I have been bitten by the bug!

That's not to say that Consciousness is something new to me! Ever since my car accident in 1987 I have been dealing intensely with this world of the non-tangible, with intense energetic experiences and insights. What fascinates me is the ease with which Gary and Dain open up new possibilities for all participants and my own sense of ease when something within me is set free after asking questions. It's also Dain's unique ability to be the catalyst to change with the energies of bodies that has a lasting effect.

Now to me Gary Douglas is the master of asking questions. He lives and creates his life from and with question. To be the question! This opened up yet another new dimension for me for which I am forever grateful.

When we ask questions, a force opens up, especially when we don't get ourselves stuck with our expectation of an immediate answer. I have always been someone who desires an answer right away. However, that impatience is what puts the brakes on other possibilities showing up. It is also what triggered the pressure and stress I experienced because I had a high expectation of myself to solve things and get everything right. Now, I know the magic of asking questions.

Since then, a lot has changed for me, in my relationship with my husband and my business. I cannot imagine my or our life without the questions and the other tools. It is an ongoing process the unfolding of which I now observe with a lot more calm than ever before. My favorite question: "What else is possible?®"helps to perceive another point of view in emotionally challenging situations, even if I consider this question only in my mind. I often ask my employees: "What else is possible" And within two to three days they actually come up with brilliant ideas about how we could change procedures or use what's in place more efficiently. In my leadership seminars, this question is always present, very loud and clear and demanding. So much so that recently one of the participants suddenly said in a discussion with a colleague: "Well, guys, what else is possible?" Hooray. Everyone laughed. A new beginning is possible.

As you are reading these chapters, I would also love to provide you with new beginnings, new impulses, new possibilities. In this book, I combine my experience from over 25 years of consulting with the insights I gained by completing the training to become an Access Consciousness Facilitator with Gary Douglas and Dr. Dain Heer and attending many other seminars and telecalls with them. These approaches will never be complete.

I am writing this book because in almost all Access Bars seminars I have people ask: "Tell me, how can we learn to ask questions in everyday life?" In subsequent seminars such as "The Foundation®" transforming questions are asked and handed out in extensive class materials and audio files for participants. But not everyone wants to wait until the next class, and in this book, you will find a lot of questions.

And now, be ready to be surprised.... What else is possible?

2. The Energy Behind the Questions

What if the answer to any question you ask can be received by you? This may happen instantaneously after you ask your question or may take a little more time to arrive. What if the answer was shown to you directly or indirectly, by an encounter, an occurrence or a coincidence? Literally something coming to you from an unexpected source. What if then you could open up an infinite source of possibilities by questions? Would you take advantage of this?

What is this question thing?

Let us first have a practical look at which questions are possible in general. So what kinds of questions are there?

Polarity Questions: yes or no are the only answers you can give to polarity questions. Are you hungry? Do you want to go see a movie? Will you take the garbage out? In this case, it's not about getting more information but rather about getting approval or also refusal. After that, the scenario might unfold in a different way. So these kinds of questions are not very instructive, they are final.

Now to Open Questions. An example: For several years I worked as a consultant for an automotive company, i.e. a car parts supplier with several locations in Germany and Austria. During staff appraisals about situations where something had gone wrong the very first question that would always come up was: Why? Why did this happen to you? Why haven't you paid attention to this before? Why are you late so often?

If you will now get a sense of this for yourself: What do those questions do with you? What is your inner reaction to them?

This is a kind of question that is constantly used - not only in the professional area but also in partnerships and families. Why have you not studied? Why are you dawdling? Why don't you have time for me? Why have you made me wait?

Do we ever get a real answer to these questions?

This is a form of question that, when addressed to me, induces a reaction of justification. I either become more intense or get angry. When Gary Douglas is asked: Why do you do XYZ, he answers: 'Because I can.' Or: 'Because I feel like it.' He smiles when saying this. And that's it.

So all questions including: Why? How come? For what reason? What for? Are investigative questions aimed at satisfying the need to find a cause. They are often used in journalism. In the technical world of Total Quality Management, which in most cases has been adapted from Toyota and their KAIZEN approach to a constant improvement of all processes and procedures, it is normal to ask why a machine standstill came about or why too many defective parts have been produced. I realized that managers are using exactly the same approach with their employees. Because they want improvement in this area as well. However, people are not processes, machines, or procedures. And what kind of energy gets created with this kind of question? Enthusiasm for change or frustration?

Even when we ask ourselves: Why does this keep happening to me? Why do I always end up with the wrong type of woman, the wrong type of man? Why am I constantly sick? Why is there never enough money? Do we really get helpful information when asking these questions? On the contrary, they will rather give rise to self-pity; make us immerse ourselves even more deeply in emotions. The whole situation becomes heavier rather than lighter.

Different, open questions, however, open up a wide range of answers for us which very often contain vital information. Questions that help us get ahead most of the time start with: What? How? Who? Where? Which?

· "What can you imagine could be different here?"

· "What would a desired outcome look for you?"

· "Who could help with this?"

· "Where could we find the most up-to-date information?"

· "What could improve the situation?"

· "What can I do different here?"

· "Which possibilities have we not yet discovered?"

In this case, it is not only our thoughts that go on the search but also our subconscious will help us. And it's exactly that which then allows for new possibilities to show up. Which of those possibilities we consequently choose however, is an altogether different story.

About ten years ago I had the opportunity to listen to several of Prof. Dr. Ulrich Warnke's lectures. The way he linked the scientific with the intellectual and spiritual realms to bring them to life fascinated me. Especially two sentences stuck in my mind: Everything we think, every thought is instantaneously – that is, without any delay – present in the entire universe. That means that virtually everyone has access to our thoughts, and we have access to all other thoughts. And: The results of a research trial vary according to the researcher's mental expectations.

This brings us to the findings of quantum physics which deals with the interaction of the smallest particles. But don't worry, I am not going to go deep into that topic now. This is only to help to us recognize our infinite possibilities. In quantum physics, results have been attained that ran counter to the assumptions of physics that had been valid up to that point. On the smallest level, matter and energy/vibration supposedly cannot be identified separately any more and consciousness has immense influence. One of the findings of quantum physics is that by observing something we change it through our attention. Very much like professor Warnke put it.

Let us proceed on the following basic assumptions:

- Everything is connected to everything.

- Everything is vibration in different frequencies.

- Consciousness creates reality.

- Energy follows attention.

- If you direct your attention at something you change it, i.e. if you change the way of observation, the object of observation changes as well.

What are the implications for us?

If you ask different questions about an issue that you are concerned about both the issue and the possibilities to deal with it change. The issue itself might not seem as hopeless any more. Maybe you will get cues in dreams. Or you have the infamous 'coincidences' happen: People you haven't seen for ages suddenly cross your path and make a remark, a call out of nowhere gives you new impulses, your gaze is attracted to an ad or a poster with a key word that helps you, and much more. Because both our thoughts and our subconscious are energetically connected to all information that exists, if you ask absolutely open questions like, "What else is possible?" – they serve as invitations to present you with a banquet of possibilities. Now it's up to you to be aware of, and choose from them.

When Martin and I were looking for a house to live in together, I would search in the newspapers for plots and houses every weekend. We wanted to create a space in which we could live together as well as work with our clients and employees. This was the only specific idea we had. We went to see various objects and places.

One day Martin said: This way we are not going to find it. I replied: How else then? What else can we do? He said: By trusting in chance. We know what we want to live like. So either we are going to find it or it is going to find us. We simply have to be in the question of: What's the best place for us?

In order to look at the exact colors of a new brochure I wanted to have printed I drove to a repro printshop outside the city we lived in back then. My navigation system guided me over hills and meadows along the woods to a small mountain village called Ehrstädt. As the landscape fascinated me, I asked in the printshop whether there were any plots to be had. The rest is history. Since 2005 we live in our ecologically built house on the fringe of the forest and are delighted at the people that come to see us from all corners of the world.

Questions open up possibilities. With each choice you make from these possibilities you gain new awareness. This is why there is no right or wrong choice. There is a choice that feels harmonious in the given moment or not. And from that choice, awarenesses evolve. Which in turn expand our capacity to perceive. And an expanded perceptive faculty opens the door to consciousness.

What is it that you desire? Being conscious?

As you read the following chapters and work with the questions set out therein I want to invite you to create your own questions as well.

There will be questions you might answer yourself right away. There will also be questions about which you can take a lot of notes because they are also designed as an invitation for you to gain clarity in your ideas and thoughts. And there are many "transforming questions" waiting for you. This is the kind of wording used in Access Consciousness. Actually, it's almost never about the seemingly evident problems or issues. These kinds of questions are aimed at bringing up the energy behind or underneath an issue, which is what it's probably really about on a deeper level. So every time you read: "What energy, space and consciousness can you be to..." you don't have to think about it cognitively. This question, as well as all the other "transforming questions", are phrased in such a way as to circumvent the logical mind and invite your subconscious to go on a discovery trip. What could this bring you?

Right after these transforming questions you will find the following phrase: Are you willing to destroy and uncreate that? This addresses your inner willingness to actually let go of unconscious energies that might constitute an obstacle on your way. Maybe you are wondering about the term: "uncreate". Everything we think up, consciously or subconsciously, is a creation. We create something. And with this phrase we want to undo that which has been created. Imagine that you have written down or drawn something on a white sheet of paper with a pencil. Now you take the eraser and erase it. What will remain? A white sheet of paper that can be used to write something else on it, so what will you write now, consciously choosing something new?

3. Self-determination vs. Other-directed

Let us start right from the beginning with what's the most important thing in the world. That is you. You are an infinite, wonderful being that has much more knowing and wisdom than you can imagine. What if you knew you could never fail? What does that feel like?

What if you knew that you have a choice in every moment, in every second, to invite into your life what you would like to have? I hear you think something like "YES, BUT my husband, my children, my job, my financial situation...". Yes, but. This "but" deprives you of all possibilities. "Yes" in this case maybe means "That would be nice", or "I would love to" – and the "but" suggests the unfeasible, the inconceivable. With the little word "but" you destroy all possibilities.

What if you knew that more than 90% of your thoughts didn't really originate in you? What if these thoughts were old patterns? Passed down from generation to generation and hence repeated time and again, charged with the energy of your ancestors, so that they have eventually become your reality? What if these thoughts simply were condensed, obsolete mental structures of collective energy fields, which we log into again and again without realizing we are doing so because it is "normal" to think this way?

Which questions have you not asked yet? Questions that might lead your thoughts in a new direction and your consciousness to expanded dimensions? When you ask a question you allow yourself to create the life you desire.

What is it that you desire? What could you be so hungry for that you would do anything to implement it?

Do you have any spontaneous ideas when I ask this? I know a lot of people who will answer: "I don't want XY any more," "I want to quit smoking," "I don't want extra pounds on my hips," "I don't want to be in debt any more," "I don't want to be bullied in my job anymore," "I am afraid to lose my partner," "I am afraid to become sick like others in my family".

So where is the focus here? On that which we don't want any more! And that which you focus on, i.e. where your mental power is directed, gets energy. This energy will make that very thing increase. It increases the creative power until it becomes a reality. This is tantamount to a self-fulfilling negative prophecy. "See, I told you I wouldn't succeed...". That means it doesn't matter if you believe in achieving something or not achieving something. You will always be right. And if you think counter to something that you want to eliminate this way it cannot work.

So let's not wait any longer. If you like you can start right away with a redirection of your mental power and invite your creativity to do so. Start now to step into self-determination, regardless of your background, regardless whether your environment has been difficult, has supported you or inhibited you until now. It doesn't matter. You can start now and every day anew, finding out what you like, how you want to live, what you want to try out.

What could keep you from doing that? That you don't know yet what exactly you want? That you don't know yet how it works? The point of view that you first have to know exactly how something works before you can start doing it is a collective pattern that consequently takes away self-determination and makes you other-directed. It doesn't allow for mistakes. It doesn't allow you to try it out yourself and discover something great and new while doing so. It's this other-directedness that tries to keep you small in order to keep you in normality. "Do only what everybody else is doing so you don't stand out".

When will you feel like determining yourself? When will you feel like recognizing which wonderful abilities you have? When will you feel like bringing the gift you are into the world?

Is now the time?

I suggest writing down everything that comes to mind right now:

> *Which questions have you not allowed yourself to ask that if you asked them would allow you to create the life you desire?*

Whatever comes up for you now, write it down. There is no right or wrong, nor good or bad. There is only this moment and whatever goes through your mind right now. Just leave it as it is. Don't do anything with it. Just allow yourself to ask questions.

It is an art to simply ask a question and not do anything with it or find an answer right away. If the answer is vital it will come.

What else is possible?

4. Letting Go of Judgment

Judging, assessing and comparing are limiting habits. This is the way we give everything we see, hear or somehow overhear a sticky label. How many labels do you think we come up with every day? This is good, this is bad, this is right, this is wrong, this is too big, this is too chunky, that person is stupid, she is making a stupid face, that is a dumb answer, this is brilliant, this is mega cool, this is great. No matter how we call it – all of these are judgments. What effect does this have on us? What effect does it have on you in particular?

Are you ready for an experiment? Okay. Just get what it feels like when you think: He's an idiot. What she's saying is absolutely wrong. This situation is so messed up....

What does that feel like for you? Does it feel light? Or does it feel heavy? Or neutral? Free? Or contracted?

What feeling would you like to have? And what can help you get out of this judgment pattern?

Transforming question:

> Everything you have unconsciously made solid within you
> in respect to judgement, that you have taken on and are
> perpetuating as a habit, instead of looking at what is, are
> you willing to destroy and uncreate that? Yes?

For me it has been and still is extremely helpful to realise the cause for judgments and evaluations. Where exactly do we start judging?

It is a succession of several unconscious thought patterns that very quickly, in a matter of split seconds, rush through our brain and our emotions. Very often we have the following loop go on:

We have a certain picture in our minds regarding a certain topic, a thing, a situation or somebody's reaction. An idea of what it is supposed to be. It has to be this way and no different. We project this idea onto the other person and already imagine how he or she is supposed to react. Let's say, for instance, you have a picture in your mind about what Christmas is supposed to look like. You imagine, among other things, that your partner will open the wine bottle in time before dinner so that this nice wine, which has been picked specifically for the occasion, will have enough time to breathe. You take it for granted that they would do that. It's normal to do this. So you don't even think about putting this idea of yours into words. You simply expect this from him. As a man, you will probably have a similar expectation of her, also unspoken.

So, what's happening in this moment?

Idea: The wine is opened, decanted and ready in time. Projection: It is normal to do this in time and for the man to do this. Expectation: He knows what I want so he will do it.

Oops. Didn't work. The wine is still not opened. The guests have already arrived. Food is being served.

What happens now? Your disappointment – that is, your "dis-illu-sionment" regarding the illusion that things will go the way you had imagined them in your mind – sparks judgment. "How annoying. Couldn't he have remembered to do that?" And since this judgment goes on internally and maybe also verbally behind closed doors in the kitchen there will often be rejection in conjunction with an energetic withdrawal. In other words, an inner distance that affects the mood; in the worst case scenario, also the mood of everybody else.

This is only a small example of what happens so often. Relationships are a fertile ground for judgments, as are companies between executives and employees and amongst employees. Executives have expectations with respect to their employees because certain things are normal to them. Many times these expectations are not verbalized because they seem "normal". And afterwards, there are angry discussions or full-blown arguments because somthing didn't go as expected. But what is normal, and for whom? Even more so with so many different generations in a company who all have a different mindsets.

People judge people because they do something in another way than they themselves would do it. And if somebody has low self-esteem they will judge themselves because they don't meet the expectations of other people. This will be even more intense in a field involving different cultures where even more deep-seated values, patterns and rituals are at play.

For the sake of illustration, here is the loop in a nutshell:

Idea, projection, expectation, judgment, rejection that can express itself in distance and withdrawal but also in emotional outbreaks, open fights or work to rule....

Sometimes, the sequence of these inner states can also change. It's quite possible for there to be rejection as a first inner reaction to an unfulfilled expectation. And only after that there is a conscious judgment that might be expressed as a reprimand or grumbling, like: "You never do this...", or "Each time I want something from you, you...." or something along those lines. And only after that distance and withdrawal will follow.

What is going through your head when you read this? Does that sound familiar? Actually, it's rather amazing to see what we will come up with in order to find fault with each other, get short range satisfaction or the hope of some relief, but this will most probably be at a high cost. In any case, we lose life energy in the process and stop being joyful.

So each time you start judging in your mind or even perceive resistance you can go through this loop and find out which ideas you bring into the world without voicing them. Because one more key is: "Say what you want so you can get what you want. Nobody can guess what's going on in your head."

So you can ask yourself:

·   What is the cause of my judgment about others? Which expectation have I not voiced?

·   What is keeping me from expressing as a wish what I truly want?

·   What could I do different next time that would help me to not go into rejection, withdrawal or emotions?

·   What expectations by others do I want to meet? Do I truly want that or am I aligning even if I don't want to?

·   With regards to whom do I have expectations and wishes that I feel uncomfortale expressing? What do I truly want, what sexual needs are there, what desires for attention or recognition, or anything else?

·   Which question could help me get out of judgment right away?

Transforming questions:

How vital, real and important have you made your judgments, your withdrawal and your rejection to make them more real to you than the capacity of your internal perception? Everything that is, are you willing to destroy and uncreate it? Yes?

How often do you go from your projections and expectations, that are based on your experience, to rejection and judgment instead of telling yourself: Okay, what's really going on here and what is different than what I think to be true? Everything that is are you willing to destroy and uncreate it? Yes?

How many expectations and projections are you using to make sure you can judge and don't produce success? Everything that is are you willing to destroy and uncreate it? Yes?

How many projections and expectations are you creating in order to make sure you fit into society, what keeps you from having awareness and consciousness? Everything that is are you willing to destroy and uncreate it? Yes?

What have you made so vital and real about projections, expectations, evaluations, judgments, rejection and distance that keeps you from choosing to live to the full, because while you are doing projections, expectations, judgments, rejection and distance you have eliminated any possibilities apart from these? Everything that is are you willing to destroy and uncreate it? Yes?

And how else could you let go? Maybe by adopting a stance in order not to go to an idea or judgment in the first place? Live and think in the here and now?

We can look at it like a meditative ZEN practice: Whenever you think you know something let it go. Whenever you are certain of something let it go. Whenever you judge somebody let it go. Whenever you judge yourself let it go.

If you cannot simply let it go, as it is practised in ZEN, you can simply replace it by: Interesting point of view I have this point of view.

As a result of remembering the "interesting point of view" you put yourself in a position to view situations or things from another perspective. Whenever you insist on being right about something or make yourself solid or are certain about something, this will help you take a fresh look at things as if you didn't know anything. And from there, new possibilities arise. Doors open. A Roman philosopher once said: "scio, nescio", meaning "I know that I don't know anything". That was his attitude in life.

So what's the point here? If we practice asking these questions and letting go continuously we won't be as stressed any more in many areas of life. When we realize that we actually never know everything on a cognitive level we step into a new space:

· We don't have to get angry if somebody behaves in a way we don't like.

· We don't have to be afraid if things don't unfold the way we had originally envisaged or hoped for.

· We don't have to have all the answers. Instead, we can be curious and ask many questions.

· We don't have to enter into an intensive war of "I am right" with everyone around us.

· We gradually begin not to judge other people any more. This way, we can open up for what they are and have good relationships.

· We don't need to control everything. Instead, we can provide helpful support without wanting to control the outcome.

The advantage of using these open questions and the approach of letting things go by applying the "interesting point of view" is a higher level of calm in the face of any situation. We can still give our best but won't be stressed out if things don't turn out the way we had planned. Thus, we are free to open the door to other possibilities, which we are not otherwise capable of perceiving.

With this approach, an unencumbered being is the result. I noticed for instance, I can be very busy but being involved in my business is not a burden to me anymore. Today I deal with things that evolve differently with more ease and I am no longer sad if they turn out differently. Usually it's conditioning through judgments we are subject to, such as: one has to work long and hard in business, things have to go as planned etc. If we look beyond that and develop new independent thoughts regarding any situation, we get out of societal conditioning, the conditioning that has created problems in the first place.

And it's from here that comparisons arise, which also keep us stuck in judgment. "What body size do you have? How much do you weigh?" Then you go and find your ideal weight in the table, a comparison that doesn't necessarily do something positive for your mood. Why compare? There are 7.5 billion people on this earth. And nobody is absolutely like another person. Comparing yourself serves to make you "alike". What for? Only to see whether you are better, worse, wiser, healthier, faster or at least as fit as somebody else? You are unique. YOU are unique. You are wonderfully unique. What if you allowed yourself to bring this uniqueness to the world?

You can ask yourself:

- What is my uniqueness that I could bring into the world?

- What am I especially good at?

- What do I love doing, designing, creating, that nobody else can do like me?

- What have I unlearned that I was once good at because I believed it's not worth anything or wasn't needed?

- What could I spend doing the whole day because it's so much fun?

Transforming questions:

Everything, on a conscious or an unconscious level, that keeps you from seeing, living and expressing your uniqueness, are you willing to destroy and uncreate that? Yes?

How many projections and expectations are you using to create the judgments, comparisons, the withdrawal and the rejection you are using against yourself? Everything that is are you willing to destroy and uncreate it? Yes?

What have you made so vital, real and important about hiding behind others, making yourself small and comparing yourself, instead of living your greatness and showing up as yourself? Everything that is, are you willing to destroy and uncreate it? Yes?

How many projections and expectations do you have about how something has to be that keeps you in a constant state of judgment and rejection of you? Everything that is are you willing to destroy and uncreate it? Yes?

Everywhere you are comparing yourself to others in order to judge yourself, to make yourself more than them or make yourself wrong, in order to get the attention you could be getting if you were being you, are you willing to destroy and uncreate all that? Yes?

Everywhere you are afraid of taking up something totally new because you have never done it before and have no comparison within you whether you are succeeding or not and you don't trust your inner wisdom but rather want to look for answers outside, are you willing to destroy and uncreate that? Yes?

If any unexpected situations arise for me I don't ask anymore how others would deal with them. I ask myself:

- What is this supposed to tell me?

- What's the purpose of what is happening right now? Do I actually have to know it?

- What exactly is it? That is, without making it bigger, worse or irrelevant?

· What can I do, be or think different in order to find new approaches?

· Who or what can assist me?

After that I can take a new look at the situation.

And each time I succeed in being completely without evaluation, judgment and comparison I can truly see what's in front of me. This moment of a deeper perception of the unexpected is magic, or even mystical!

5. Body, Health, Aging

What if the state of our body and our health were predominantly determined by the points of view and attitudes we have about and toward them? That would mean that when it comes to aging it is not so much about the number of life years but what we think about aging and what attitude we adopt toward it. What if it was us who could determine to a large extent how healthy we are, and how we can become healthy and stay young?

Latest scientific research suggests we should extend our perception of the world in this direction as well.

The following story, which had far-reaching consequences for my life will illustrate the benefit such a point of view can have for recovery and wellbeing.

It's a Friday afternoon around 4 pm when I decide to drive home earlier than usual from my office at interRent in München-Laim. Sometimes I stay there until 10pm in the evening or later. But today I have planned a free evening in my beautiful flat for a change. Shortly after Brunnthal highway traffic suddenly comes to a halt and I barely manage to brake and come to a stop just a few centimeters away from the bumper of the car in front of me. A shudder runs through my body. How lucky have I been? Lucky! My gaze falls onto the rearview mirror. Oh – no! A red car hits me and swerves to the left shoulder. The impact propels me with great force onto the car in front of me. Oh my God! From behind, at an even greater speed, a white vehicle rushes in my direction, a third collision. I feel how I am being flung back and forth in my seat, until everything around me becomes quiet.

How long am I sitting there? No idea. At some point I get out of my car and am being asked whether everything was okay. "Yes, yes, no harm done" I hear myself say. The police have already arrived and I note down my name and the circumstances of the accident. When I get home and look at what I have written I can hardly decipher it. Who wrote something there?

My head hurts. A tearing pain goes through my whole back. Maybe I should go and see a doctor? Yes, maybe tomorrow.

On Saturday, I am advised at the emergency department in Bad Aibling to immediately go to hospital. I have multiple injuries with whiplash from the cervical spine down to the tailbone. No, I won't go to any hospital. I return home, go to sleep and know I will drive to Munich on Monday. As soon as I arrive at internist Dr. Ortner's practice in Schwabing, he says: "I won't send you to hospital, they will only mess you up". He takes everything into his hands. In the most literal sense: over the course of several weeks he restores me, vertebrae by vertebrae, using chiropractic treatment, acupuncture, homeopathics and hands-on processes. And that was back in 1987!

And he doesn't leave it at that. He recommends going to a seminar by Mantak Chia, a Chinese master. I learn from him how to stimulate and direct my life energy by breathing techniques and mental focus. Hot rushes tear through my spine and tears stream down my face. There is indescribable pain in my whole body as the energy spreads throughout it. At the same time, I am being permeated by joy and light. Words cannot describe these sensations.

Anybody I talk to about this thinks I must be out of my mind. Not to go to hospital is considered rather irresponsible. And acupuncture and meditation exercises are humbug anyway.

I am practising this technique daily. The pain goes away. Thanks to my doctor's empathetic treatment and the precise instructions by

Mantak Chia my spine becomes straight again, the disc prolapse dissapears and my life totally changes.

Today, in 2017, there are many more people who know about these techniques and their effects. Not everyone, but certainly a larger number of people.

Our body feels firm and solid but is it, really? Contemporary science also shows that the body consists of vibrating molecules and that in between these molecules there is energy and space. Our thoughts and our way of life influence how these molecules behave; Lighter or heavier?; Vibrant or stuck?; Flexible or rigid?; Permeable or blocked?; Swirling or linear?; Communicating or excluding? Any mental and physical information we give our cells causes them to act on it.

There is an interesting book by Dr. rer. nat. Klaus Volkamer called "Die feinstoffliche Erweiterung unseres Weltbildes – Ansatz einer erweiterten Physik zur unbegrenzten Gewinnung Freier Energie aus der Feinstofflichkeit" (The Subtle Extension of Our Perception of the World – An Approach of Advanced Physics to Unlimited Generation of Free Energy from Subtle Matter). In it, he describes that our physical health is determined mainly by subtle matter-related factors and explains different energy fields in this context, our gross body is superseded by a subtle body that runs it. This subtle body field is informed by our thoughts and experiences. At the same time, this subtle body field is in resonance with other fields - either the subtle body fields of other people or the global morphogenetic field.

He calls the subtle body fields of different groups of people collective fields. These collective fields, in turn, contain specific information. Collective fields distribute their information to all members, i.e. to all individual subtle body fields of each person, as long as there are resonance options. What does this imply for our daily life? If we are in a group of people, at work, in our families, on holiday, in a seminar, and we agree with other people's points of view or reject them we are in resonance with the respective information. Yes, even when we are rejecting them, we are still connected to this collective information field because antagonisms or rejections also create resonance – full of resistance. All of this influences the individual subtle body field that governs the physical body. That means that our body reacts to any subtle matter-related information that we ourselves initiate by our thought patterns and that we take on through the collective field – either by agreeing or resisting. We can also call this collective consciousness. Given permanent contact, this collective consciousness has an entropic effect, to use the scientific term, meaning it is detrimental to our health and stress-inducing.

The global morphic field, however, has a 100% negentropic effect, meaning it is beneficial for our health. Dr. Volkamer writes on p. 235:

"Through intense contact of A (subtle body field) to the global field B, which has a purely negentropic effect, however, spontaneous healing is possible which medicine cannot explain today. In a less pronounced form so-called A/B contacts can be induced by mental alignment with the global negentropic field, even only by way of a conversation with a doctor of choice, that have placebo effects for which there is no explanation as of now either. Finally, the global morphogenetic negentropic field B contains complete information for perfect health stored on a subtle level that's only waiting to get a chance to flow into the subtle body field."

How do we get in touch with this morphogenetic negentropic field that is conducive to health and effects healing on all levels the more often we connect with it? Possibilities to do so include healthy sleep, regenerating rest (for example, bars and body sessions, see appendix for more information), daily meditation and a continuous renewal of our own thought and belief patterns that allow us to get in touch with other fields and manifest beneficial information in our body.

Let's start with the latter. Maybe you want to write down your thoughts about your body?

·   What is my body to me?

·   How do I experience myself in my body?

·   How much do I honor my body?

·   What do I like about my body?

·   What do I dislike about my body?

·   How much fun do I have with my body?

·   How do I see myself: too fat, too thin, too wrinkled, too nice?

·   What do I generally think about my body?

·   How flexible am I?

·   What do I love about my body?

·   Who am I mimicking with my body?

·   Which thoughts provoke stress in me?

·   Whose thoughts and points of view do I take on in general?

·   What or who am I rebelling against?

·   Who or what do I reject?

·   What lies am I choosing in order to create my body the way I am creating it?

·   What emotions am I using to create my body the way I am choosing to create it?

·   What other questions can I ask myself here?...

Transforming questions:

Everything you have done to not create your body the way you would like in order to not create your life the way you would like, will you destroy and uncreate that now? Yes?

All the belief systems you have taken on with respect to diets that keep your body from actually changing, will you destroy and uncreate that now? Yes?

How many of the judgments about yourself, about how you and your body cannot be, are judgments that actually create your body? Everything that is, will you destroy and uncreate that now? Yes?

How many conlcusions do you engage in in order to create your body the way you are choosing? Everything that is, will you destroy and uncreate that now? Ja?

All the assumptions you have about yourself and what's bad about you that make you create your body the way you create it, none of which is true, will you destroy and uncreate it all now? Yes?

What have you made so vital, valuable and real about all the structures and the order of how your body should function that keeps you from allowing the living chaos from which your body functions that would induce a total change of your body from within, and of you together with it? Everything that is, will you destroy and uncreate that now? Yes?

Health

When do you think you are healthy? When do you think you are ill? What if all of this could be indications for you how you could think differently or where you could choose to stay or what you could maintain or change?

When I followed my inner knowing after that car accident and consulted my internist I had a premonition that something would occur here that would really help me move forward without knowing what it was. I didn't give in to the belief patterns of my environment but found a solution for myself beyond what's "normal". What would it mean to you if you trusted yourself, adopting a new, open attitude towards yourself, and forged your way?

Questions you can ask yourself about health:

· What do I think about my health?

· How much rest do I allow myself? How many times-out do I allow myself? How much activity do I allow myself?

· Which beliefs or thoughts do I have about healing? What impact does that have on me?

· Whose beliefs regarding illness or health am I taking on? What impact does that have on me?

· Whose points of view am I taking on with respect to nutrition, fitness or sports? What impact does that have on me?

· What could be conducive to my health?

· What do I really feel like doing?

· With whom could I talk about health and healing power?

· Do I believe that my body can heal itself?

· Do I believe that I can heal myself?

· What could I start doing in order to support my body and my health? What could I do less of or quit altogether?

Transforming questions:

> What have you made so vital, valuable and real about the assumptions about healing or non-healing that keep you and your body from creating what your body and you are capable of? Everything that is, will you destroy and uncreate that now? Yes?

> Everywhere you have given up the choice to create your body and your health and have looked to the order of society or the rules of institutions in order to conform will you destroy and uncreate that now? Yes?

> How many lies about health and healing have you taken on that keep you from receiving, perceiving, knowing and being? Everything that is, will you destroy and uncreate that now? Yes?

Aging

What does aging mean to you? In our collective, there are many different patterns. There is a period of time in our lives in which we most likely will have been told: "You're not old enought for that yet. You are too young to do that". So what might have been "implanted" by this? Aging more quickly.

Many are happy when they finally turn 18. But already when THREE is the first digit in our age, some start to panic: "I am already thirty and not married yet". Accordingly, everyone has their own issue with different digits at the beginning of a number of years. And depending on which environment we are in, the number might also indicate things that are "normal" with respect to that age, like for example: "Yes, at forty of course your eyesight will deteriorate". Or: "I'm already fifty-five; that means I won't change anymore". I often hear this statement from executives. Or: "In my family, both my mother and my grandmother had high blood pressure in old age. That means I need to be careful now". Or: "I have only seven years left until my retirement". Well, great, and then what?

This is why I still like Udo Jürgen's song (Udo Jürgens was an Austrian-Swiss composer and singer of popular music born in 1934, who wrote this German classic in 1977; translator's note) so much: „Mit 66 Jahren, da fängt das Leben an, mit 66 Jahren da hat man Spaß daran". (rough translation: "At 66, your life will begin, at 66, you will enjoy it")

What thoughts do you have about aging? The more aware you become of your beliefs around this the easier it will be for you to change them. So, if you like, write down:

· What thoughts do I have about aging?

· What do I believe about getting old and staying young?

· What patterns are there in my family regarding aging and staying young?

· What do I believe about death and dying?

Transforming questions:

Wherever you have been so stupid as to destroy your body, to make it age and make it ill in order to conform to other people's realities, will you destroy and uncreate that now? Yes?

What have you made so vital, valuable and real about overwriting the consciousness and intelligence of your body and everything it desires to be, with other people's emotions, feelings, thoughts and assumptions, in order not to allow yourself to be the creative chaotic expressions of a greater possibility? Everything that is, will you destroy and uncreate that now? Yes?

What energy are you not willing to be that, if you were willing to be it, would create everything your body and you desire to be? Everything that is, will you destroy and uncreate that now? Yes?

What else is possible?

6. Money

What does money mean to you?

Most people have trouble around money their whole life. They either spend too much, or they never have enough of it, or they go into debt, or they have money and fear losing it. Whatever it is, we create a lot of stress by this and reduce our life quality. I used to do the same to myself.

When in the late 1980s I sat in the second front row at an event in Brussels and watched Anthony Robbins stand on stage three days in a row, full of energy with hardly any breaks and work with 1700 people in the audience I know: "I can learn a lot from him!" This third day is also the reason why I whip out two credit cards in the evening and book the Master University. Nine days spent with him on Hawaii and several more days spent in San Diego with him and his team follow. Without knowing where the money I am spending will come from, I realize, I must do this.

I have a monthly payback agreement with 10% interest in place with the credit card companies. That seems to be doable. And at the same time it puts a lot of pressure on me. When I finally have to figure out how to pay for the flights and accommodation to the seminars I have booked because all credit cards are maxed I know: This needs to change. I don't want to live on borrowed money any more.

I keep asking myself: "What can I do different? What can I change? How do I acquire assignments? Who could I ask? What am I good at that I would like to do more of?"

I am constantly asking these questions, in the morning, at noon, in the evening. I am not courageous enough to make company acquisitions by phone. I much more prefer to have a face-to-face conversation. And I also don't have a name yet in the consulting area or doing leadership seminars because this is my first year as a freelancer. So how to make progress here and make up for the deficits?

At that time, I am organizing Tao Yoga seminars for the Chinese master Mantak Chia in Munich and Vienna and simultaneously translating his words and lectures from English to German. I am blossoming. When Brita from the Frankfurter Ring asks me whether I would like to work as an interpreter for him in Frankfurt as well I happily agree. From him I learn Tai Chi, Chi Gong, meditation and other systems, which up to this day are a daily contribution for me. They allow me to enhance or build up my energy at any time. The money I receive for interpreting and organizing the seminars help me pay for rent, food and insurances, at least. But not a cent is left over to pay off my debts.

During one of those seminars with Mantak Chia in Vienna a married couple approaches me who owns a publishing house and is also self-publishing a consumer journal. A wonderful connection begins. I can write articles for this newspaper, which helps introduce and expand the seminars. The number of participants grows and consequently the profit as well which is not huge yet but constantly increasing. And that's not all. I get the opportunity of supporting the publishing house employing all my sales and leadership capacities, which I have gathered and aquired in my previous positions in various companies. And Tony Robbins' seminars also contribute to me adopting new points of view regarding leadership topics and values. His coaching which is based on the INSIGHTS analysis provides me with totally new insights about behavioral aspects and lays the groundwork for further powerful encounters and a new business. My life is expanding. Now I am able to gradually pay back the above-mentioned 10% and I am very careful not to use a credit card any more. When finally all my accounts show a black zero I experience immense relief.

And I keep being in the question: "What else can come now? How to proceed? What do I really desire to bring to the world? What do I want to be successful at? How can people benefit from the fact that I exist?"

So what do I want to say with this? Is it really about money? If there is a lack of money, then yes, it is. But is it really the money itself that is lacking? What is your attitude towards money? What do you think about money? Because, and here lies the key. It's not as if there was no money in the world, right? It's about the way you get access to it. Is money the problem, or rather you and your attitude towards it?

Your financial situation often sparks judgments, conclusions and decisions. "I cannot afford xy." Do we accept lack by saying this? Or: "I don't earn enough." Is that true? Or is it an interesting conclusion that could be interpreted in different ways. Such as: "I am not worth it or my work isn't worth it or I am not putting in enough effort?" Or: "When I will do better financially, I will...". This is an interesting linkup as well. Because this way, a causal dependance is created that is out of your hands and might come about at some point – or not.

In order to gain clarity for yourself you might want to answer the following questions:

· What does money mean to me?

· What keeps me from possessing it?

· Is it easier for me to spend money or to create money?

· What feelings do I have with regards to money?

· What would I really love to do the whole day?

· What brings me a lot of joy?

· What am I good at?

· What's right about me having no money or not enough money?

· What can I bring to the world?

· What could I create that would bring me money?

· What ressources do I have available?

· Who or what could help me?

What if you had the capacity to create a different reality for you? What if your current financial situation or the situation you grew up in was totally independent of this? Would you like to start creating something different?

Transforming questions:

Everything that keeps you from getting total clarity about this, will you destroy and uncreate that now? Yes?

What would you need to choose as your personal reality that you are currently not choosing, in order to be the rich, creative receiving person you truly be? Everything that doesn't allow that to show up, will you destroy and uncreate that now? Yes?

What feelings are you using to create the fears, concerns or loss around money you are choosing? Everything that is, will you destroy and uncreate that now? Yes?

All your projections, expectations, separations, rejections and judgments as well as all the refined judgments you have around money, will you revoke, recant, rescind, reclaim, renounce, denounce, destroy and uncreate those? Yes?

All your projections, expectations, separations, rejections and judgments as well as all the refined judgments about money that you have taken on and made your own, will you revoke, recant, rescind, reclaim, renounce, denounce, destroy and uncreate them? Yes?

Another interesting point of view we have about money is that we have to give up something in order to be able to take or get something. Let us look at what we normally say: "Give and take".

What does this imply? I give something and take something in return that has a value equal to what I have given. If we follow through on this thought that means: "If I don't give anything I also cannot take anything." Or: "I only take approximately as much as I have given." Or: "I only give as much as I have received." This is where we have the principle "tit for tat"/an eye for an eye and a tooth for a tooth", don't we?

Could you imagine somebody wanting to pay more for your service, your being, your book or your conversation than you currently consider it to be worth? Would you be willing to receive that? Or would you immediately have an impulse or a bad conscience and have to give something again in order for it to balance up?

All of these are points of view we have taken on that keep us being governed by others, and dependent. These points of view often originate from experiences in our childhood, which parents and other people have shown as an example or propagated in mutliple facets.

What if you could simply receive whatever comes your way? What if you could embrace "gifting and receiving" and thus always remain open to whatever wants to come to you at any moment? What if this could make you feel rich?

You could ask yourself:

· Where in my life do I always look for balance?

· When is it uncomfortable to have something gifted to me?

· How does it affect me if somebody shows me appreciation?

- In which situations do I expect to get something back because I have given something?

- How do I feel when I gift something?

- What if I gifted something and suddenly had a gift for me come from a totally different direction?

- What if I gifted attention and didn't expect anything?

Transforming questions:

What energy, space and consciousness can you and your body be that would allow you to receive everything that came your way? Everything that doesn't allow that, will you destroy and uncreate that now? Yes?

Everywhere where you have destroyed and rejected the principle of gifting and receiving in favor of the principle of giving and taking in this reality, are you willing to destroy and uncreate that? Yes?

What have you made so vital, valuable and real about giving and taking as if it were the only possibility to survive in this reality? Everything that is, will you destroy and uncreate that now? Yes?

What financial reality have you mimicked or what financial reality have you refused or what financial reality have you eluded in order to avoid having this financial reality, and thus created it? Everything that is, will you destroy and uncreate that now? Yes?

Everywhere you have decided that money is the source of all your problems and that only money can get you out of all your problems, will you destroy and uncreate that now? Yes?

What else is possible that you don't even dare to imagine?

7. Sales

The little red lamp lights up and the recording starts. Now the role-play begins. I sit opposite of my client. "Mr. Müller, I am glad we are meeting today. You are interested in including the new PC in your product range. It has the interface that allows you to connect to mainframe computer systems as well. The screen is 12 inches wide. You have the option to choose different keyboards. I would like to recommend XY as its touch...".

Do you know salespeople like that? I was rather off (judgment ☺), back then. We had been taught to stress, above all, the products' advantages. Now my world was being turned upside down. Now there is a new trick: "The person asking questions is the leader or If you don't ask you can't lead".

Even though it's still about selling, new perspectives open up all the same. "What are your ideas, dear customer? How much do you want to invest? What is your intention for the future beyond that? What are your plans with this regarding staff training?"

Suddenly it becomes interesting to learn more about the person sitting in front of me. And as if by magic my amount of turnover changes. When previously I had left after what I had considered a good presentation in which I had presented all my capacities and my point of view and all kinds of solutions, I was often taken by surprise when a few days later I received polite rejections: "You were absolutely convincing with your presentation, but we will make another choice".

That was in the 80s. What has actually changed since then? My interest in other people grew. I became curious to get to know their viewpoints and to see the world through their eyes. "Wow, that's interesting, so you can look at it this way, too?" And if you can look at it this way as well, what other possibilities are there? A deep change had been affected, not only with regard to sales, but also and most important of all, in my subsequent executive positions. I didn't tell people any more how things are done. Well, only sometimes. I asked my employees, and keep doing so unto this day; 'how can things be done?' and what ideas do they have? This approach is also crucial as a consultant, trainer and coach.

At some point I got that in sales, it's not about your argumentation. It's really about being someone who it's fun to exchange views with, develop new things with and consequently do business with. It is a totally different world and a much more lively one.

Maybe you will want to ask yourself:

· Where am I trying to sell something? And how do I do that?

· When did talks go successful? What exactly did I do then?

· When have conversations and talks not been successful? What was different then?

· What approach, what attitude did I have when entering the conversation?

· What expectations did I have with respect to the result of the conversation?

· What posture did I assume during the conversation?

· How did my body feel in general during this conversation?

· What did I think about my dialogue partner? Before, during and after our conversation?

Another very important question could be:

· What can this person receive from me?

And this question is not only helpful in sales situations, but also when leading people or in relationships. What's important in every conversation is the willingness to receive. Maybe you also know this from private conversations? You tell somebody something, and all of a sudden the other person turns around or gets distracted by somebody else? And everything you say afterwards somehow comes to nothing?

Well, then your dialogue partner was not set on "receiving mode". Or you have told him or her something they weren't included or interested in. You have sent something without knowing the correct address. There was no invitation for an exchange.

A successful conversation can take place whenever you find out through questions what's interesting to the other person. Let them talk and then see which of your offers or capacities will serve their interest.

Transforming questions:

> What energy, space and consciousness can you and your body be to enter into conversations with total openness, awareness and ease? Everything that doesn't allow that, will you destroy and uncreate that now? Yes?

> Everywhere you're pretending to have the other person's best interests at heart but are actually thinking about your own success, are you willing to destroy and uncreate that now? Yes?

> Everything you have initiated, consciously or unconsciously, in order to put inner evaluations about others or the situation in which you are above your capacity for free perception and hence to perceive what is, will you destroy and uncreate that now? Yes?

Nowadays digital media play an increasing role in the area of sales. It is those who not only function as vendors but as a real partner for the client that can stand out from the host of offers and information.

Do you really want to reach your clients? Then you can go beyond offering a ready solution.

What does that mean? Ask them questions that allow them to find a way for themselves. How can they realize themselves what, about your product or service, is helpful for them?

Maybe you want to ask yourself first:

·   What is the benefit of my product/my service that goes be-yond the immediate benefit?

·   What questions could I ask?

·   What does the product or service mean to me personally?

Transforming questions:

What can you be or do different to have ease with your environment? Everything that doesn't allow that, will you destroy and uncreate that now? Yes?

How many parts of you have you given up in order to con-vince others of something or because you wanted to make them happy? Everything that is, will you destroy and un-create that now? Yes?

What energy, space and consciousness can you and your body be that would allow you to conduct talks and do business from a pool of time-proven experience and new creative ideas? Everything that doesn't allow that will you destroy and uncreate that now? Yes?

8. Relationships

A client who feels lonely after her divorce comes to me for coaching sessions. She is good-looking, has an open heart and a lot of energy. She sincerely wishes for a partner that would appreciate her qualities and share life with her.

Many of us harbor this desire for a deep relationship and the hope that the other person will truly understand and "get" us. Wouldn't it be simply wonderful to have an intimate relationship evolve with this person? Maybe there is the idea of simply meeting this person, blending with them and henceforth being totally fulfilled?

What if we recognized that it is exactly this idea that is in the way of us actually experiencing what we wish for?

What if everything we required to be happy and fulfilled was within us?

What if all the requirements for being fulfilled were here right now, in this very moment, and not only in an imaginary, ideal future?

Is it possible that the idea of an ideal partner and the anticipated satisfaction and fulfilment were only a phantastical wish, which alone doesn't allow us to find what we are looking for?

In actuality, those of us who have a partner or have had one know that living together brings about experiences we could never have imagined. There are nice and not so nice surprises, tensions, arguments, distance, and sooner or later, reconciliation. In reality, fulfilent usually doesn't come from the other person but by us becoming active or opening up to have it. And then, all of a sudden, we experience the sought-after resonance with the other person as if by a miracle!

In every partnership there will always come that moment, sooner or later, when the fog parts which has allows us to see our own wishful fantasy in the other person and how we will live out our magical attraction together. The increasing clarity that one can now look at the other, or ideally, both can look at each other and see what is, can bring about disenchantment, maybe even disillusionment (in the sense of dis- illusion).

Some couples break up at this point going: "I was wrong about you, I'm sorry, that's it now..." This is what also happened to the client I have mentioned in the beginning. This time of solitude now gave her the opportunity to get to know herself better, to perceive her true requirements and preferences and to become more self-reliant and confident. On this basis she can now gear to a new partnership where the chemistry is right and the partners' lifestyle harmonizes.

Other couples adjust and endure, despite an increasing distance, for the children's sake, because of their shared apartment, their reputatation, their profession...

In the best case scenario the partnership will grow into a real and sustainable relationship. By changing the wishful thinking, evaluations and expectations that have been projected at the partner so far, a productive space opens up allowing for true understanding, real love, appreciation, profound eroticism and mutual complementation on the basis of two independent beings forming a bigger unit.

Which of these options are you choosing? Or what constellation are you involved in right now?

What would it be like if we gave up the fantasy of a partner who will fulfill us, that this fantasy of a better future that can only be brought about by another, and any other related hopes, wishes and dreams? What could evolve if instead, we focussed on creating a fulfilled here and now with ourselves? Which then allows for a real and harmonious resonance in a relationship?

You could ask yourself:

- What fantasies do I have with regard to a partner?

- What could help me look at my hopes, wishes and dreams realistically?

- Which are the utopian ideals that I imagine and hence, where am I constantly lying to me and deceiving myself?

- Which relationships have I experienced as fulfilling?

- What has made other relationships fulfilling?

- What was my contribution to this state of fulfillment?

- What exactly did I do or not do when this fulfilling moment was there?

- What could I do more or less of in this respect?

- What could I start doing?

- What could I stop doing?

- What ended the state of fulfillment?

A basic question would be: "How can I develop a fulfilling relationship with myself in order to be capable of creating and living fulfilling encounters with another person (people)?"

What causes fulfillment? My experience has shown me time and again that the focus on pleasures such as food, entertainment, TV, internet, alcohol, sex and drugs only brings temporary satisfaction. Many times you feel empty afterwards, have a hangover or you want more and more.

Fulfilment, as I see and perceive it, springs from deep personality layers. This could mean finding something in life that is meaningful to me, that by my being something becomes possible for others that hasn't been possible before. This is when moments of gratitude occur, it becomes possible to enjoy the beauty of the moment, to feel erotic attraction, to experiene a flow in the body and simultaneously experience expansion, treat others lovingly and be grateful to have a partner, siblings or employees who are a contribution to my life – although and maybe even because they are challenging sometimes.

You could ask yourself:

· What is it that fulfills me?

· What can I be to experience the exhilarating moments even more intensely?

· Who do I love?

· Where in the world could I be a contribution that would fulfill me?

· What could I intensify in order to expand the wish to serve myself and also be useful to others?

· What inner relationship do I have to myself?

· What inner relationship do I have to others?

· What can I do to perceive my constant connection and relationship with everything around me even more clearly?

· What can I change now to feel fulfilled?

It is helpful to answer these questions not only in your head but also in writing. It helps me to get out of never-changing thoughts going round in circles, and sometimes surprises me how this leads to a new creative path almost by itself that brings with it a blissful feeling of happiness. Maybe you will be surprised at how much you are already doing and what you can add in order to generate happiness from within. I know from the coaching sessions I treat myself with, how much clarity and 'aha' moments come from this. Something is brought from the subconscious to the conscious. And only then is there a possibility to change something.

If these questions were the key to attract the partner who is truly harmonious for you, would you choose that?

Transforming questions:

> What energy, space and consciousness can you and your body be to be in harmony with that which is harmonious for you? Everything that stands in the way of that, will you destroy and uncreate that now? Yes?

> Which refinded judgments are you choosing that keep you from choosing the relationships you could be choosing? Everything that is, will you destroy and uncreate that now? Yes?

> What have you made to vital, real and important about your definitions about relationships that keep you from creating a new reality with respect to relationships? Everything that is, will you destroy and uncreate that now? Yes?

> Everything you are doing to prove that you are good while in actuality you are treating other people badly, will you destroy and uncreate that now? Yes?

> How many of your judgments are you hiding and refusing to have inner allowance for, that are having a continuous effect and creating what you want to avoid? Everything that is, will you destroy and uncreate that now? Yes?

> Everywhere you have chosen judgments instead of awareness, will you destroy and uncreate that now? Yes?

> What have you made to vital, real and valuable about all the excuses you are creating that determine that you

cannot change anything, ever, and which keep you from creating your life and your relationships beyond your limitations? Everything that is, will you destroy and uncreate that now? Yes?

What else is possible?

9. Diffculties, Conclusions, Control

When in 2004 my PR consultant Sabine organises a talk for me as a keynote speaker, I am absolutely thrilled to be able to talk in public about energy and consciousness.

Martin has created a video showing pictures of our honeymoon in California with energetic surfers, powerful waves, green-blue nature and also with me doing Tai Chi exercises against the backdrop of the rising sun on a flat plateau on "Mount Chesta".

Those powerful and moving pictures as well as the carefully selected music he had put to the video served to tune the listeners in to my talk in an almost meditative manner. There is a lot of excitement and curiosity as I enter the stage.

On the bistro table at the right far end of the stage there is my laptop and the draft of my speech concept lies in front of it. Usually I only use notes and have the guiding thread in my head when I speak. Usually I go back and forth on stage, keep moving and interact with people. Today it's different. The whole talk is written up, word by word. Sabine thinks it is vital to stick exactly to this order. I am glued to the bistro table, keep looking at the script and use the mouse to click through the power point presentation. I feel rigid. My self-consciousness is decreasing by the minute. Only when I ask a member from the audience to come up on stage to do a kinesiologic test, when I deviate from the carefully scripted structure and find my way out of the controlled speaking and follow my nature again does the liveliness return a little. After a short applause I leave the stage. Never again will I do it this way!

Difficulties are designed to show you when you have chosen against you. In this situation, I had completely chosen against me and had succumbed to another person's control.

Difficulties make you see that you can choose again, different and for yourself in such a way that an expansion of what currently is will become possible, beyond judgments. You have the opportunity to change anything. After a short while I terminated our association, our points of view were too far apart.

It's important to know that everything you have ever chosen, consciously or unconsciously, will become evident as a result. Things do not just happen. Keep remembering that you are the creator of your reality.

Ask yourself:

· What is causing difficulties for me right now?

· What am I currently judging as a problem or a difficulty?

· What have I set in motion by my decision that now appears as a difficulty to me?

· When have I agreed to something that didn't seem so important at the time that now I see its result or effect appears as a problem to me?

· Whom do I see as difficult and why?

Maybe you can perceive, if you replay certain situations in your mind's eye or can perceive them emotionally, that situations defined as a difficulty always go hand in hand with an inner judgment. What else is possible instead? Look at the situation as it is, don't add anything, don't make it bigger with emotions than it is.

Don't read anything into it, what could have been and what still might happen. And don't diminish it or ridicule it.

Ask yourself:

· What exactly is this?

· What have I not seen that I could see now?

· What possibilities do I have to change this in another direction that are harmonious?

· Can I do it myself or, if not, with whom?

· What else is possible now that hasn't been possible before?

That which makes it almost impossible to change a difficulty or a difficult situation are conclusions. A conclusion means the death of any possibility in most cases. Manifested conclusions are fixed points of view someone has about a certain topic. This person will fight for their rightness, for being right. He or she will want to have their opinion validated or implement it - at any rate. You can recognize a conclusion if someone says: "That's the way it is. I am right.", "This is not possible because...". "We know this will function this way, because we have already made this experience." "This is not possible, because it has already been tried once and didn't work back then." And there are many more statements in this vein. Often, these conclusions will be followed by the corresponding reasons and justifications. "I can't..., because...." Does that sound familiar?

My experience on stage had locked me up so much that I actually decided not to speak in public any more. But deep down inside I knew that I had to. So I gradually shed my reservations again.

If you find yourself confronted with similar conclusions in your environment or tend to come to conclusions yourself you might make it a habit of staying in the question. For example: "Aha, that's interesting. What else is possible?" Or "Oh, great that you have already tried something, what else could you try?" Or "What if we just played with some ideas here to develop something else?"

Ask yourself:

· What topics do I have a fixed point of view about?

· Where am I willing to come to a quick conclusion?

· In which areas of my life do I adopt other people's conclusions?

· How could my life change if I didn't come to conclusions any more?

· What conclusion do I not want to give up by any means?

For many years, I had this belief in me: "I always have to do everything myself." Wow, what in intense conclusion! And that's exactly the way it showed up. A self-fulfilling prophesy. And if nevertheless someone would show up to offer their help, guess what was my ready answer? "Thank you, I'll manage".

And this is where oftentimes control comes into play. Control is what we do to influence situations by fixed opinions and ideas in a way we would like them to be. Or we feel that somebody else wants to control us. More often than not the reaction is rejection, withdrawal, resistance against anything that comes from this person.

When we are in control mode – either exercising control or being in resistance to it – we cut ourselves off from receiving yet again. We cannot get what we actually want to have, because we have shut down our perception of the possibilities by the solidity of the control or the resistance against control.

When I had gotten myself into control on that stage by the written-out script and the position of the bistro table, my perception, my sense of the audience disappeared. I was dull and not perceptive to the signals that I usually can see on people's faces. And this was why I didn't react spontaneously to them as I normally automatically do when I am speaking without a script. The control to speak exactly the way I had written it down destroyed what I love most.

Ask yourself:

· What am I controlling and for what purpose?

· Where do I believe I will fail without control?

· What do I want to control in my partnership?

· What am I controlling with respect to my children, friends and relatives?

· Where and when do I feel controlled? By whom?

· What does this control do to me?

· How do I react to control?

Transforming questions:

> What energy, space and consciousness can you and your body be to be out of control, out of linearity, out of concentricity at all times and to be the creative chaos you truly be with total ease? Everything that doesn't allow that, will you destroy and uncreate it now? Yes?

> What have you made so vital, valuable and real about the conclusions that keep you from seeing the possibilities you could be choosing? Everything that is, will you destroy and uncreate it now? Yes?

> What difficulties do you create in order to prove to yourself that you are capable of solving any difficulties that are supposedly getting in your way? Everything that is, will you destroy and uncreate it now?

10. Creativity and Life Forms

On my sideboard, propped against the wall like a painting, sits a book. It's the German first edition of 1996 of "Sacred Mirrors – The Visionary Art of Alex Grey". This book contains colorful mystical pictures about being human that have evolved from inner images and visions. And just today as I am writing this chapter, I've read an interview in the Swiss Psi-Journal with artist Alex Grey who was born in 1953 in the United States, translated by Sabin Sütterlin. What a coincidence!

Alex Grey is asked: "Can you give readers any advice how to awaken their own creative potential?" Alex Grey: "Creativity is not a rare thing at all. Everyone is inherently creative. You can't escape from it because it's all that's going on." And another quote: "If there is only ONE and it is all of us, we are the creative force that brought forth the universe on day one. We are One with that force."

Maybe you want to ask yourself:

· What do I want to create today?

· What could I invent today that no one else before me has invented?

· What book, which film, what music is an inspiration to me?

· What idea would I like to pursue?

· With whom could I make a date to have a talk?

· What Divine Spark wants to manifest through me?

- What is my creative power?

- What have I not dared yet to commit to paper or express otherwise?

- What if I expressed my creativity in a dance class, a book club, an art class, a cooking class, a singing lesson?

- What would really be fun for me to create, apart from all my other activities?

- What could I surprise myself with today?

And what does that mean: life forms?

When I attended Gary Douglas' Foundation class in Australia in May 2015 we also addressed the topic of creativity. He recommended writing down all ideas and thoughts in a journal or notebook dedicated specifically to that purpose, anything that comes to mind, anything that might become a project. Really... anything.

A few days later, Martin and me are in New Zealand. We are strolling along the harbor. I get the impulse to go into a huge tourist shop. Martin asks: What do you want there? "To buy myself a creativity book", I grinned. No sooner said than done. Already by the evening the first ideas were jotted down in there. Two days later, I am yet again attending Gary's class – "Choice of Possibilities"– (previous known as Level two and three).

"Gary" – I have the courage to take the mike – "Gary?"

Gary: "Yes?"

Me: "Gary, I have bought an ideas book and already written down a lot."

Gary: "Oh, great!"

Me: "Yes, but there are so many ideas that I don't know when and how to do all of this???"

Gary: "That's a conclusion. Too many ideas – I won't make it. And what do you end up doing then?"

Me: "Well, nothing at all."

Gary: "Correct."

Me: "So what else can I do?"

Gary: "Any idea you write down, any project you start, any book you want to write, any song you want to compose – all those ideas have their own life form. The very moment you conceive them, they have their own life. Also ask them when they want to come into existence. You can ask them when is the best time for them. You can ask them, for example, when they want to be written – if it's a book or a play. Then you might work on them several days in a row. Suddenly they don't appear in your focus anymore and don't tell you to continue working on them. That's when a break is needed. Maybe because you will get new information in the meantime or another project will have priority for several days. Simply listen to what the projects or ideas are telling you."

And ever since I've been doing it exactly like this. Sometimes I feel as if I am bursting with ideas. Then I think – where's my creative book? And put them down right away. I take a look in this book everyday and am in communication with them. This way, they come into life one after the other and also very often simultaneously and parallel.

What could be helpful for you to have your own creativity come forth even more?

Transforming questions:

> What have you made so vital, real and important about the idea that you could only do one after the other, and

first had to finish one thing before starting something new? Everything that is will you now destroy and uncreate that? Yes?

Whereever you've had others convince you that you are not creative and therefore haven't dared to simply try something out for the fun of it, are you willing to destroy and uncreate it? Yes?

Whereever you believe you don't even need to begin doing something because you don't know enough about it or you aren't perfect enough anyway and you won't complete it anyway are you willing to destroy and uncreate that? Yes?

What energy, space and consciousness can you and your body be to openly receive impulses, choose from them what you want to implement, and then do it? Everything that is keeping you from that, are you willing to destroy and uncreate that? Yes?

What if any obstacle that is showing up for you was an opportunity to develop your creativity and strike a new path? Everything that is keeping you from that, will you destroy and uncreate it now? Yes?

11. Questions in the Morning

What if you could start your day already in the morning with drive, joy and ease? What if you could be curious about what will come, about what you will create? About the people you are going to meet? What can you create today?

Sometimes, before actually waking up, I spend a few more minutes in bed – stretching myself luxuriously. Then I feel like a cat just awoken from its slumber that is bringing back to life all limbs. And then, questions come up inside of me:

- Who or what do I want to be today?

- What brilliant ideas and thoughts will I commit to paper today?

- What can I do for myself to be in a high vibration?

- Who do I love and who loves me?

- What is possible today that I haven't even considered yet?

In order to motivate your positive inner mood you can also sing sentences or chant them like a mantra. For example:

- What brilliance will I bring to the world today?

- Which divine inspirations will take me further now?

- What magic will show itself to me today?

- Universe, what miracles can you bring me today?

- What beautiful experiences will I receive today?

- In which way will the great relationship I have with myself show up today?

- How will I experience joy and ease today?

- What would it take to create everything that is already waiting in me to be created?

- How can I master today's challenges with ease and elegance?

- What questions can I ask today in order to give everything a new spin?

- Which infinite possibilities will come to meet me today?

- What can I choose today that will enhance my possibilities?

12. Questions and Clearings in the Evening

Many times when we are already lying in bed Martin will ask me: "What was the most beautiful thing for you today?"

I then wait for a moment and have all the pictures come up in my mind that have moved me; The intense conversation with him on the couch. The way we merged with each other afterwards; that call from a client with good news; a transformational coaching; my walk through the forest where I watched a deer graze....

Whatever it was, it will end the day with this nice, light feeling.

So what questions could you ask yourself?

· What was special today?

· What has worked out really well today?

· What was an inspiring encounter?

· Who or what made me laugh?

· What am I grateful for?

· What have I managed today in a creative manner?

· If I were to live the past day again what would I choose?

· What would it take to be able to experience a certain situation of this day with more ease?

- What magic could cause progress in a certain area?

- In which way could a problem solve itself elegantly?

And what else ...?

In order to let go of all other attached energies that might keep my subconscious busy I say some clearing statements:

- What long-term complex project have I been involved in today, including both progress and setbacks? Everything that is I destroy and uncreate it now.

- What has hurt me today? All the energies I am sensing here, and all the feelings I am adding myself, I now destroy and uncreate.

- Whom have I observed as alienated or adverse today? Any related interpretations, conclusions or definitions I now destroy and uncreate.

- What would I do different next time? Anything that doesn't allow that I now destroy and uncreate.

- All the energies, thoughts and emotions that make me unconsciously attach to topics of family, clients, friends or other encounters of the day, I now destroy and uncreate.

- What energy, space and consciousness can me and my body be in order to sleep deeply and wake up absolutely regenerated? Everything that doesn't allow that I now destroy and uncreate.

What question could you ask yourself?

13. The Clearingstatement

„The Clearing Statement

With permission from the authors out of the book: „The Ten Keys To Total Freedom" by Gary M. Douglas and Dr. Dain Heer.

In Access Consciousness, there is a clearing process we use to destroy and uncreate blockages and limitations.

Here's a brief explanation of how it works:

The basis of the universe is energy. Every particle of the universe has energy and consciousness. There is no good energy or bad energy; there is just energy. It is only your judgment that makes anything good or bad. Energy is present, mutable and changeable upon request. It is the substance by which transformation occurs. Everything you say, everything you think and everything you do generates what occurs in your life. Whatever you choose puts the energy of the universe, the energy of consciousness, into action— and that shows up as your life. This is what your life looks like in this very moment.

Point of Creation, Point of Destruction

Every limitation we have was created by us somewhere throughout all time, space, dimensions and realities. It involved making a judgment or a decision or taking on a point of view. How and why the limitation was created does not matter, nor does any other part of its story. We only need to know that it was created. We call this the point of creation (POC). The point of creation energetically includes the thoughts, feelings, and emotions immediately preceding the decision, judgment or point of view we took on.

There is also a point of destruction. The point of destruction (POD) is the point where we destroyed our being by taking on a decision or a position that was based on a limited point of view. We literally put ourselves into a destruct universe. The point of destruction, like the point of creation, includes energetically the thoughts, feelings, and emotions immediately preceding the destructive decision.

When you ask a question about a blockage or limitation, you call up the energy that has you locked into it. Using the clearing statement, you can then destroy and uncreate the blockage or limitation (as well as the thoughts, feelings and emotions connected to it). The clearing statement allows you to energetically undo these things so you have a different choice.

The Clearing Statement

These are the words that make up the clearing statement:

Everything that is, times a godzillion, destroy and uncreate it all.

Right and wrong, good and bad, POD and POC, all 9, shorts, boys and beyonds.

You don't have to understand the clearing statement for it to work, but if you wish to know more about it, there is additional information in the glossary.

With the clearing statement, we are not giving you answers or trying to get you to change your mind. We know that doesn't work. You are the only one who can unlock the points of view that have you trapped. What we are offering here is a tool you can use to change the energy of the points of view that have you locked into unchanging situations.

To use the clearing statement, you simply ask a question designed to bring up the energy of what has you trapped, including all the crap built on it or hiding behind it, then say or read the clearing statement to clear the limitation and change it. The more you run the clearing statement, the deeper it goes and the more layers and levels it can unlock for you. You may wish to repeat processes numerous times until the subject being addressed is no longer an issue for you.

How Does the Clearing Process Work?

Asking a question brings up an energy, which you will be aware of. It's not necessary to look for an answer to this question. In fact, the answer may not come to you in words. It may come to you as an energy. You may not even cognitively know what the answer to the question is. It doesn't matter how the awareness comes to you.

Just ask the question and then clear the energy with the clearing statement:

Everything that is times a godzillion, will you destroy and uncreate it all? (Say yes here, but only if you truly mean it.) Right and wrong, good and bad, POD and POC, all 9, shorts, boys and beyonds.

The clearing statement may seem nonsensically wordy. It is designed to short-circuit your mind so that you can see what choices you have available.

If you could work everything out with your logical mind, you would already have everything you desired.

Whatever is keeping you from having what you desire is not logical. It's the insane points of view you wish to destroy.

The clearing statement is designed to fry every point of view that you have so that you can start to function from your awareness and your knowing.

You are an infinite being, and you, as an infinite being, can perceive everything, know everything, be everything and receive everything. Only your points of view create the limitations that stop that.

Don't make it significant. You're just clearing energy and any points of view, limitations or judgments you've created. You can use the full clearing statement as we've given it here, or you can just say: POD and POC and all the stuff I read in the book.

Remember: It's about the energy. Go with the energy of it. You can't do this wrong. You may find that you have a different way of functioning as a result of using the clearing statement. Try it. It may change everything in your life."

Read or speak the Clearingstatement after each transforming question to have even better results.

Acknowledgments

I am full of gratitude for Martin, my husband. To me, you are a partner, lover, friend, creative source and constant catalyst, as well as sometimes a midwife to my wishes expanding, express myself, change and LIVE freedom.

My gratitude also goes out to precious companions and instigators: Dr. Thomas Ortner, Master Mantak Chia, Anthony Robbins, Gary M. Douglas and Dr. Dain Heer. Your being has changed and enriched my life.

I am also very grateful for my sisters Dagmar Barth, Karla Schellhammer and Gabriele Nimsky-Magnussen. Exchanging ideas with you is always valuable to me.

Thank you, Peter Hörnstein. You are a bastion of calm and back me up in our office. Your enthusiasm and dedication make all those creative ideas come to fruition in this reality.

What else is possible?

Appendix

How to proceed now? What if you considered additional possibilities to make your life even easier?

The following events allow you to continue on your path with me and Martin and free yourself even more:

Coaching – for yourself, as a couple or in a team

Some say you just have to have the willpower to get out of stuck situations or reach a certain goal.

But there are situations or encounters with other people in which we are inhibited, don't feel good, make unnecessary mistakes, create loss or simply are at our wit's end. And this is when all our best intentions and even efforts come to no avail, although we have tried so hard.

Would a coaching with us be helpful in this case?

We do our coaching as an art of support and counseling based on appreciation. External obstacles and inner experiences are given space to be voiced and looked at from a different angle. Body language, sensations, subconscious thoughts and dreams, questions and feedback take us on the path of/get us on to useful contexts and new solutions.

The uniqueness of each client's singular situation is being acknowledged, and we create an adequate helpful setting that brings about insight, strengthening and change come about.

In order to enhance the questions laid out in this book you can try out new perspectives and put the experiences you make doing so in perspective together with us, in a healthy and future-oriented manner. This way, clarity, new chances and changes will be effected. A new, more comprehensive understanding will emerge that allows you to think, feel and act differently.

Access Consciousness Seminars

The basis of Access Consciousness are the "Access Bars®".

The Access Bars® are the energetic key to be able to allow and implement the changes you desire for your life with ease and grace, by "doing" less and starting to "be" more. Learning this method leads you exactly to this goal. Beate and Martin Nimsky show how you use the Access Bars® for different areas of life so you can receive them yourself and gift them to other people. Possible topics are, for instance, healing, control, communication, creativity, aging, sexuality, money and more.

It is an reconstructive/structuring and relaxing process that allows you to leave all your limitations that you want to change behind you.

The Access Consciousness Seminar "The Foundation"

This class erases the basis of limitation from which you have thought you have to live as if you didn't have another choice! By looking at your life issues from a totally different perspective it will become easy to change anything.

You will discover the meaning of: "What else is possible?" in a new way. Your perception of yourself and the world around you will enhance, and consequently, you will recognize an unlimited number of more possibilities.

You get tools which allow you to change anything that doesn't work in your life. Your relationships will improve, including the difficult ones (i.e. also your relationship with yourself) since your capacity to integrate instead of resistance will expand exponentially.

Body processes are included as well that allow the cellular consciousness to let go of limiting information and have more ease with being in life. Things that used to be annoying suddenly don't matter anymore.

Advanced seminar after an Access Bars® class: "Access The Body" – Discover the greatness of your body

When you begin to change your relationship with your own body your relationship with all of your life changes as well. The Access Body Processes are designed to open up a dialogue with your body and create a connection within yourself that allows you to enjoy your body instead of fighting against it.

In this seminar, verbal processes and hands-on processes will be used to release tensions, resistance and energetic blocks in your body.

Please address any questions to us here:

nimsky Institut für intrinsische Kompetenz

Email: institut@nimsky.de

T.: +49 7266 915390

www.nimsky.de

www.accessconsciousness.com/BeateNimsky

Recommended Reading:

The Ten Keys to Total Freedom – Gary M. Douglas and Dr. Dain Heer
https://www.accessconsciousness.com/en/shop-catalog/book/
projections-expectations-separations-judgments--rejections/#a_
aid=A2961

Divorceless Relationship – Gary M. Douglas
https://www.accessconsciousness.com/en/shop-catalog/all/the-
tenkeys-to-total-freedom/#a_aid=A2961

Being You, Changing the World – Dr. Dain Heer
https://www.accessconsciousness.com/en/shop-catalog/all/di-
vorceless-relationships/#a_aid=A2961

Projections Expectations Separations Judgements & Rejections –
Gary M. Douglas
https://www.accessconsciousness.com/en/shop-catalog/book/be-
ing-you-changing-the-world/#a_aid=A2961

-CPSIA information can be obtained
at www.ICGtesting.com
Printed in the USA
LVHW012117181022
731002LV00009B/144

9 781634 931823